THE SECRET GARDEN

by Frances Hodgson Burnett

For over sixty years, the story of *The Secret Garden* has charmed readers of successive generations.

After losing her parents in a cholera epidemic in India, Mary Lennox, an unloved, unattractive and awkward little girl is packed off to Misselthwaite Manor on the bleak Yorkshire moors. Here she encounters Ben Weatherstaff, the crusty old gardener, Dickon, the young boy who befriends her, and eventually her invalid cousin Colin, a spoiled and arrogant child who meets his match in Mary. Together they are drawn into the magical world of animals and nature around them and gradually – like the hidden garden they discover and nurture – Mary and Colin are both transformed by the beauty and mystery they find there.

Graham Rust's illustrations for the *The Secret Garden Daybook* first appeared in *The Secret Garden* by Frances Hodgson Burnett, published by Michael Joseph Ltd., in 1986.

Conceived and produced by
Breslich & Foss, Golden House,
28-31 Great Pulteney Street, London W1R 3DD

Designed by Roger Daniels

First published in Great Britain by
Piatkus Books, 5 Windmill Street, London W1P 1HS

ISBN 1-871054-05-2

The SECRET GARDEN DAYBOOK

illustrated by

GRAHAM RUST

Diamond

JANUARY

1
2
3
4

5

6

7

8

9

10

JANUARY

11

12

13

*The carriage lamps shed
a yellow light on a
rough-looking road
which seemed to be cut
through bushes and low-
growing things which
ended in the great
expanse of dark
apparently spread out
before and around them.
A wind was rising and
making a singular, wild
low, rushing sound.*

JANUARY

14

15

16

17

18

*Almost the next moment
a wonderful thing
happened. She heard a
soft little rushing flight
through the air – and it
was the bird with the red
breast flying to them, and
he actually alighted on
the big clod of earth quite
near to the gardener's
foot . . .*

19

JANUARY

20

21

22

23

24

25

26

27

28

29

30

31

FEBRUARY

1

2

3

4

5

6

She had just paused and was looking up at a long spray of ivy swinging in the wind, when she saw a gleam of scarlet and heard a brilliant chirp.

FEBRUARY

7

8

9

10

11

There was a laurel-hedged walk which curved round the secret garden and ended at a gate which opened into a wood in the park. She thought she would skip round this walk and look into the wood and see if there were any rabbits hopping about.

12

13

14

15

FEBRUARY

16

17

18

19

20

21

22

23

*. . . it was an old key
which looked as if it had
been buried a long time.
Mistress Mary stood up
and looked at it with an
almost frightened face as
it hung from her finger.
'Perhaps it has been
buried for ten years,' she
said in a whisper.
'Perhaps it is the key to
the garden!'*

FEBRUARY

24

25

26

27

28

29

MARCH

1

2

3

4

5

6

7

MARCH

She was standing inside
the secret garden . . . It
was the sweetest, most
mysterious-looking place
anyone could imagine.
The high walls which
shut it in were covered
with the leafless stems of
climbing roses, which
were so thick that they
were matted together.

MARCH

8

9

10

11

12

13

14	
15	
16	
17	
18	Our Wedding Anniversary (1995)
19	

MARCH

20

21

22

23

24

25

26

27

28

29

30

31

APRIL

1	
2	
3	
4	

5

6

7

8

9

10

11

12

13

14

15

16

17

18

19

20

APRIL

A boy was sitting under a tree, with his back against it, playing on a rough wooden pipe. He was a funny-looking boy about twelve. He looked very clean and his nose turned up and his cheeks were as red as poppies, and never had Mistress Mary seen such round and such blue eyes in any boy's face.

21

22

23

24

25

26

27

28

29

30

When she stepped to the wall and lifted the hanging ivy he started. There was a door and Mary pushed it slowly open and they passed in together, and then Mary stood and waved her hand round defiantly. 'It's this,' she said. 'It's a secret garden, and I'm the only one in the world who wants it to be alive.'

MAY

1

2

3

4

5

6

7

8

9

10

MAY

11

12

13

14

15

They went from bush to bush and from tree to tree. He was very strong and clever with his knife and knew how to cut the dry and dead wood away, and could tell when an un-promising bough or twig had still green life in it.

16

MAY

17

18

19

20

21

22

23

24

25

... and under the apple-tree was lying a little reddish animal with a bushy tail, and both of them were watching the stooping body and rust-red head of Dickon, who was kneeling on the grass working hard. 'This is th' little fox cub,' he said, rubbing the little reddish animal's head. 'It's named Captain.'

MAY

26

27

28

29

30

The moor was hidden in mist when the morning came, and the rain had not stopped pouring down. There could be no going out of doors.

31

JUNE

1	
2	
3	
4	

5

6

7

8

9

10

JUNE

11

12

13

14

15

16

Swiftly something flew across the wall and darted through the trees to a close-grown corner, a little flare of red-breasted bird with something hanging from its beak . . . 'It's part o' th' springtime, this nest-buildin' is,' he said. 'I warrant it's been goin' on in th' same way every year since th' world was begun.'

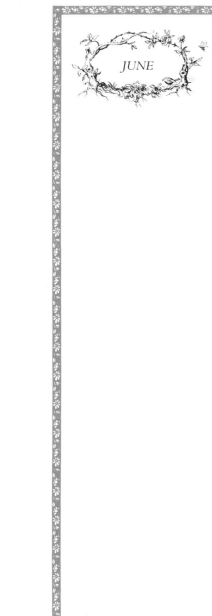

JUNE

17

18

19

20

21

22

23

24

25

26

27

28

JUNE

29

30

JULY

1

2

3

4

JULY

5

6

7

8

9

10

11

12

13

14

15

16

JULY

17

18

19

20

Sometimes the rook flapped his black wings and soared away over the tree-tops in the park. Each time he came back and perched near Dickon and cawed several times as if he were relating his adventures, and Dickon talked to him just as he had talked to the robin. Once when Dickon was so busy that he did not answer him at first, Soot flew on to his shoulder and gently tweaked his ear with his large beak.

21

22

JULY

23

24

25

26

27

28

29

30

31

. . . Soot took the entire half of a buttered crumpet into a corner and pecked at and examined and turned it over and made hoarse remarks about it until he decided to swallow it all joyfully in one gulp.

AUGUST

1

2

3

She had been running and her hair was loose and blown, and she was bright with the air and pink-cheeked . . .

4

AUGUST

5

6

7

8

9

10

11

12

13

14

15

16

AUGUST

17

18

19

20

And this, if you please, this is what Ben Weatherstaff beheld and which made his jaw drop. A wheeled-chair with luxurious cushions and robes which came towards him looking rather like some sort of state coach because a young rajah leaned back in it with royal command in his great, black-rimmed eyes and a thin white hand extended haughtily towards him.

21

22

AUGUST

23

24

25

26

27

28

29

30

31

Ben Weatherstaff walked behind, and the 'creatures' trailed after them . . . keeping close to Dickon, the white rabbit hopping along or stopping to nibble . . .

SEPTEMBER

| 1 |
| 2 |
| 3 |
| 4 |

Dickon held his rabbit in his arm, and perhaps he made some charmer's signal no one heard, for when he sat down, cross-legged like the rest, the crow, the fox, the squirrels, and the lamb drew near and made part of the circle, settling each into a place of rest as if of their own desire.

SEPTEMBER

5

6

7

8

9

10

11

12

13

14

15

16

SEPTEMBER

17

18

19

20

21

22

23

24

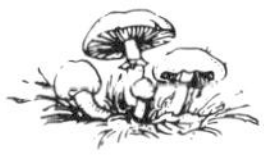

SEPTEMBER

25

26

27

28

29

30

OCTOBER

1
2
3
4

OCTOBER

5

6

7

8

9

Dickon made the stimulating discovery that in the wood in the park outside the garden where Mary had first found him piping to the wild creatures, there was a deep little hollow where you could build a sort of tiny oven with stones and roast potatoes and eggs . . .

10

OCTOBER

11

12

13

14

15

16

17

18

19

The secret garden was not the only one Dickon worked in. Round the cottage on the moor there was a piece of ground enclosed by a low wall of rough stones. Early in the morning and late in the fading twilight . . . Dickon worked there planting or tending potatoes and cabbages, turnips and carrots and herbs for his mother.

OCTOBER

20

21

22

23

24

25

26

27

28

29

30

31

NOVEMBER

1

2

3

4

5

6 The Night of the Beginning of our relationship (1992)

7

8

9

10

NOVEMBER

11

12

13

14

15

16

17

18

19

20

21

22

NOVEMBER

23

24

*The fountain was
playing and was
encircled by beds of
brilliant autumn flowers.*

NOVEMBER

25

26

27

28

29

30

DECEMBER

1

2

3

4

DECEMBER

5

6

7

8

9

10

11

12

13

14

15

16

17

18

19

*The place was a
wilderness of autumn
gold and purple and
violet and flaming
scarlet.*

DECEMBER

20

21

22

23

24

25

26

27

28

29

30

31